Titanic

Richard Musman

Titanic

Ernst Klett Sprachen
Stuttgart

Das Hörbuch zu Titanic per Klett-Augmented-App

Das Hörbuch zu Titanic kannst du per Klett-Augmented-App herunterladen und abspielen. Dazu installierst du die App auf dem Smartphone oder Tablet, suchst Titanic in der Buchliste oder über die Sucheingabe und scannst die Titelseite oder die jeweilige Kapitel-Auftaktseite, um die Audiodateien herunterzuladen.

Hinweis: Das Hörbuch zu Titanic wurde stellenweise vereinfacht und ist daher nicht durchgehend identisch mit dem gedruckten Text.

Klett-Augmented-App kostenlos downloaden und öffnen | Bilderkennung starten und die **Titelseite/Kapitel-Auftaktseite** scannen | Audios laden, direkt nutzen oder speichern

Apple und das Apple-Logo sind Marken der Apple Inc., die in den USA und weiteren Ländern eingetragen sind. App Store ist eine Dienstleistungsmarke der Apple Inc. | Google Play und das Google Play-Logo sind Marken der Google Inc.

1. Auflage   1   13 12 11 10 | 2026 25 24 23

Nachfolger von 978-3-12-542400-5
Alle Drucke dieser Auflage sind unverändert und können im Unterricht nebeneinander verwendet werden.
Die letzte Zahl bezeichnet das Jahr des Druckes. Das Werk und seine Teile sind urheberrechtlich geschützt. Jede Nutzung in anderen als den gesetzlich zugelassenen Fällen bedarf der vorherigen schriftlichen Einwilligung des Verlags.

Layoutkonzeption: Elmar Feuerbach
Gestaltung und Satz: Eva Mokhlis, Swabianmedia, Stuttgart
Umschlaggestaltung: Sandra Vrabec
Titelbild: Ullstein Bild GmbH, Berlin
Druck und Bindung: Digitaldruck Tebben GmbH, Biessenhofen

Printed in Germany
ISBN 978-3-12-542401-2

Contents

1 The Proud Departure

'The Titans, of Greek mythology, were a family of giants. White Star's great new liner, Titanic, is a giant, the mightiest ever built, a ship that Britain can be proud of. She is 300 metres long, 30 metres broad, and weighs 46,000 tons. She has been built to carry 3,500 passengers and crew and has a top speed of over 22 knots (41 kilometres an hour). The luxury for first-class passengers is quite exceptional. Artists and craftsmen have provided an extraordinary variety of styles. There is a

5

2 **Titan, Titanic** [ˈtaɪtən, taɪˈtænɪk] – 2 **mythology** [mɪˈθɒlədʒi] – 3 **liner** large boat carying people across the sea regularly – 3 **the mightiest** the most powerful – 6 **crew** people working on a boat, aeroplane etc. – 7 **knot** [nɒt] the speed of ships is measured in knots, nautical miles (1,852m) per hour – 7 **luxury** [ˈlʌkʃəri] great comfort, usually expensive – 8 **exceptional** very unusual – 8 **craftsman** specialist worker – 9 **variety** [vəˈraɪəti] number of different things

Georgian saloon, a Louis XIV saloon, a Louis XV saloon. The staircases go down four decks, with the breadth and splendour of a luxury hotel, and there is a lift. One of the wonders of the ship is that its lighting is all electric. Many of our hotels still do not have electric light. The Titanic also has a gymnasium and a heated swimming-pool.'

This is a resume of the many articles that were written about the world's greatest ship on the eve of her maiden voyage in April, 1912.

One of the most exciting pieces of information that the journalists had to report was the ship's very special construction:

'The Titanic is the safest ship in the world. She has a double bottom and 16 watertight compartments. If there is a collision and the bows of the ship are holed, her bulkheads can be shut immediately by the officer on the bridge. All he has to do is pull an electric switch. This magnificent ship is unsinkable!'

The *Titanic* was built by one of Britain's finest shipbuilders, Harland and Wolff of Belfast, and the firm's managing director, Thomas Andrews, and eight of his workers were invited to sail with her. Not one of them ever saw Ireland again.

On Wednesday, April 10th, 1912, thousands of sightseers, friends and relations came to Southampton to see the great ship off. Few ships have ever carried so many distinguished passengers. There was the American artist, Frank Millet, a well-known British journalist, William Stead, an American novelist, American senators, and some of the richest men and women in British and American society. On board, too, was the managing director of the White Star Line, Bruce Ismay, for whom it was a very great occasion.

1 **Georgian (style)** style of the 18th century in England – 1 **Louis XIV; Louis XV** styles of the 17th and 18th centuries in France – 2 **(boat) deck** floor on a boat – 2 **splendour** ['splendə] magnificence, glory – 5 **gymnasium** [dʒɪm'neɪziəm] room or hall with apparatus for sports, etc. – 7 **resume** [rɪz'juːm] summary – 8 **on the eve of** a short time before – 8 **maiden voyage** [ˌmeɪdən'vɔɪɪdʒ] the very first journey of a boat – 12 **watertight compartment** [ˌwɔːtətaɪt kəm'pɑːtmənt] separate areas inside a boat without openings to let water in – 13 **bow(s)** [baʊ(z)] front part of a ship – 14 **bridge** part of the ship where the captain stands and controls the movement of the ship – 21 **to see the great ship off** to watch the Titanic leave the harbour – 22 **distinguished** [dɪs'tɪŋgwɪʃt] important, famous – 26 **on board** [ɒn'bɔːd] on a ship – 27 **a great occasion** an important event

In fact Bruce Ismay did not quite know whether he was a passenger or a member of the crew. After the ship sailed he would suddenly jump up and rush up to the bridge, or down to the engine-room where he gave orders to the engineers without the Captain's knowledge. Yet Bruce Ismay was not nearly as sure of himself as he must have seemed to his fellow passengers.

There were also on board 500 third-class passengers, most of whom were British, Dutch and Scandinavian emigrants who were leaving Europe to start a new life in America.

As the tugs pulled the great liner out into Southampton Water, no one could possibly have believed that four days later the *Titanic* would be lying 2½ miles down on the floor of the Atlantic. After all, the *Titanic* was unsinkable, and in those days the public had complete faith in the inventive, forward-looking British industrialists. Mr Andrews, however, who wandered about the ship, checking everything with expert eyes and making notes of small things that needed changing, was a little more cautious about his ship. "Unsinkable, no!" he said. "But it'll take an awful lot to send her to the bottom."

First the *Titanic* crossed the Channel to Cherbourg, where she picked up more emigrants from the Continent. Then she went on to her last stop at Queenstown, Southern Ireland, where a boat carrying more than a hundred Irish emigrants came out to meet her. Suddenly the people in the boat gave a cry of horror. A black face was grinning down at them from one of the funnels. The superstitious Irish were certain it was the devil, and a sure sign of catastrophe. Actually it was only a stoker, who had climbed up inside the false funnel to give them a fright.

The *Titanic* nosed her way into the Atlantic, gathering speed all the time. Soon she was doing 22 knots. There were now 2,207 people on board, of whom 898 were members of the crew. The sea was calm, so the passengers were able to enjoy all the luxuries that the floating palace had to offer. The stewards and stewardesses

10 **tug** a boat with a strong engine used to pull large ships in or out of a harbour – 17 **cautious** ['kɔːʃəs] careful – 25 **funnel** [fʌnl] part on top of a ship where smoke comes out – 25 **superstitious** [ˌsuːpəˈstɪʃəs] believing in magic, etc. – 26 **catastrophe** [kəˈtæstrəfi] – 27 **false** [fɔːls] not real –
28 **fright** shock – 29 **to nose** one's way to move slowly forward – 29 **gathering speed** moving faster –
33 **to float** to stay on the surface of water (or other liquids)

were kept busy carrying coffee and drinks to the distinguished passengers in the different saloons. Some of these passengers had suites of rooms which included cabins for their personal servants. A suite of this kind cost £ 888, which in those days could have fed ten British families for a year.

Among the first-class passengers there were many American millionaires, Ben Guggenheim, John Jacob Astor, Martin Rothschild, Arthur Ryerson, George Widener. Then there was the English Countess of Rothes and Sir Cosmo Duff Gordon and Lady Duff Gordon.

A reconstructed first-class stateroom on board the Titanic

Among the second-class passengers, mostly people of moderate incomes, there was a young schoolmaster, Lawrence Beesley, who was soon to become famous as the author of a little book called 'The Loss of S.S. Titanic'.

The third-class passengers were well looked after. They had cabins with comfortable bunks, and spacious saloons. However,

---

11 **of moderate income** not rich and not poor − 16 **spacious** ['speɪʃəs] large

the White Star put third-class passengers on the lowest deck, right forward and right aft, very near the water line. The two parts were connected by a long passage, and 'to avoid trouble', they separated the unmarried women from the unmarried men, putting the men forward and the women aft.

On the evening of Saturday, April 13th, the ship's commander, Captain Smith, an experienced and much admired officer felt well pleased with his ship, as he sat in the dining-room with his distinguished guests, smoking his after-dinner cigar.

2 **aft** [ɑːft] at the back of a ship

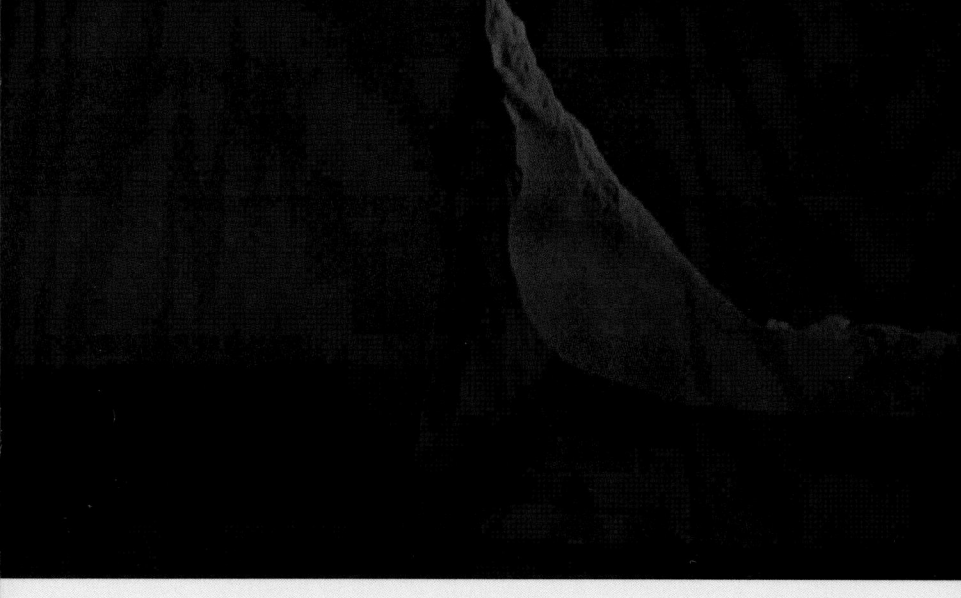

2 Iceberg Straight Ahead!

At 9 o'clock on Sunday morning, April 14th, the wireless operator, Phillips, received the following message from the Cunard liner, *Caronia*:

5   *Captain, Titanic. West-bound steamers report icebergs in 42° N from 49° to 51° W. Compliments, Barr.*

Phillips handed the message to Captain Smith while he was at breakfast in the dining-saloon. He read it through quickly and then passed it on to one of the passengers sitting at his table. He did not consider the warning important, even though the icebergs reported by the *Caronia* lay right across his course.

---

2 **wireless operator** [ˌwaɪələsˈɒpəreɪtə] person in control of the radio, receiving and sending messages – 5 **west-bound** [ˈwestbaʊnd] going towards the west – 5 **to report** *here:* to say what has been seen – 6 **compliment** *here:* best wishes – 10 **to consider** *here:* to think

Three hours later came a second warning, this time from the White Star liner *Baltic*:

Greek steamer reports passing icebergs 41° 51' N. Longitude 49° 52' W. Wishing you and Titanic all success – Commander.

5   This time Captain Smith showed the telegram to Bruce Ismay. Ismay was no more worried by it than the Captain. All he said was:
"So we'll reach the ice by tonight, then?"
"Yes, sir," the Captain replied.
There was no suggestion from managing director to Captain that
10 he should reduce speed or alter course to the south. Yet, although they did not know it, the French liner, *Niagara*, with 1,000 passengers on board, had crashed head-on into an iceberg only three days before, and on the course the *Titanic* was taking. No lives were lost and the *Niagara* reached port under her own steam. But the ship
15 that went to her help reported seeing icebergs 200 metres high.
However, few commanders in those days would have accused Captain Smith of taking a great risk. At this time of year icebergs were not considered a danger even on the shorter northern route. Lookouts were able to spot icebergs at considerable distances.
20 Should Captain Smith have been disturbed by the large numbers of icebergs reported and by their size? He was a commander of great experience. Everyone on board had complete trust in him and in the *Titanic*.
There was a reason for the exceptionally large number of icebergs
25 on the shipping routes. The Arctic winter had been unusually mild. So all along the mountainous Greenland coast the tips of glaciers had cracked in the warm temperature and dropped into the sea,

---

2 **Baltic** ['bɔːltɪk] White Star liner. All White Star liners had names ending in "ic". – 3 **longitude** ['lɒndʒɪtjuːd] *(geografische) Länge* – 9 **suggestion** [sə'dʒestʃən] idea to do sth – 10 **reduce speed** [rɪ'djuːs 'spiːd] *here:* to make the ship go slower – 10 **to alter course** [ˌɔːltə'kɔːs] to change direction – 11 **Niagara** [naɪ'ægərə] – 12 **head-on** with its head, or bows – 14 **under her own steam** *here:* without help from another ship – 16 **to accuse** to tell sb you know he has done wrong – 19 **lookout** *here:* seaman looking for icebergs or other dangers – 19 **to spot** to see – 19 **considerable** [kən'sɪdərəbl] great – 20 **disturbed** *here:* worried – 22 **experience** *here:* knowing a lot about sth – 22 **They had trust in him.** They believed they were safe with him. – 26 **tip** end – 26 **glacier** ['glæsiə] river of ice

forming thousands of large icebergs. Currents and winds carried them south into the North Atlantic, and across the shipping lanes.

By the evening of Sunday, April 14th, the *Titanic* was steaming at 22 knots and had reached a point about 400 miles south-east of Cape Race in Newfoundland. She was only two days' steaming from New York. There was great excitement on board. The first-class ladies were wearing their most beautiful dresses, the men were all in dinner jackets. Diamonds flashed on fingers and necks. The most expensive wines flowed. Even the second-class dinner menu was so rich that at least one young lady had to go to bed afterwards. In the third-class saloon the emigrants were talking excitedly about the new life they were going to begin. They had no complaints about the *Titanic*. They had not expected to be so comfortable. The Irish were having a party and dancing to the bagpipes. Pretty, unmarried girls soon found boy-friends. Only a few suffered the misery of sea-sickness, because the sea was so calm. But there was one disturbing development. The temperature was dropping. At 7.00 p.m. it was 43 °F (10 °C). By 10.00 p.m. it was 32 °F (0 °C), and by 10.30 it was 31°, which meant that the air was below freezing-point and that there might be ice not far away. Only the Captain and his officers knew this, but it did not alarm them.

At 10 o'clock the Captain came on to the bridge and told First Officer Murdoch that he was going to get some sleep.

"Call me if you're worried about anything," he said.

Then he pointed to the top of the mast.

"Tell the lookouts in the crow's-nest to keep a careful watch for icebergs."

As the Captain retired to his cabin, the ship steamed on through the night at a steady 22 knots, while up in the crow's-nest the

---

1 **current** [ˈkʌrənt] movement of water – 2 **shipping lane** particular route across the sea used by ships – 3 **to steam** to move (by steam power) – 8 **dinner jacket** black coat, worn in the evening – 8 **to flash** to shine suddenly and brightly – 9 **to flow** *here:* to pour out of – 12 **They had no complaints.** [kəmˈpleɪnts] They were satisfied. – 14 **bagpipes** national musical instrument of Scotland and Ireland – 15 **misery** [ˈmɪzəri] *here:* awful feeling – 21 **to alarm** to frighten – 22 **First Officer** second most important oﬁicer on a ship (after the captain) – 26 **to keep watch** to look carefully – 29 **steady** *here:* keeping the same speed – 29 **crow's-nest** [ˈkrəʊznest] place high on the mast where a seaman looks for icebergs or other dangers

lookouts, Frederick Fleet and his mate, kept their eyes fixed on the darkness ahead. The night was clear and the stars shone brightly. The new moon cast no light on the inky black sea, but Fleet and his mate were not worried. They felt confident they could recognize
5 an iceberg by the light of the stars. Suddenly Fleet cried, "My God! Look! There! It isn't white, but it's an iceberg all right!"

He sprang to the alarm bell and rang it three times. Then he shouted down the phone to the bridge, "Iceberg straight ahead, sir!"
10 "What's he going to do?" Fleet thought desperately, as the iceberg rushed towards them. A head-on collision seemed certain. The lookouts were getting ready for it, when very slowly the bows began to move to port. They could feel the vibration as the engines went full speed astern, but the ship did not lose very much speed. It raced
15 beside the iceberg, and the lookouts thought they had had a lucky escape. They neither heard nor felt the crash.

Down on the bridge, First Officer Murdoch heard a noise he had never heard at sea before – a tearing, grinding noise coming up from below the waterline. He knew that the ship had struck the iceberg
20 and immediately moved the switch which closed the bulkheads of the watertight compartments. A moment later the Captain rushed on to the bridge.

"What's happened?" he asked.

"We've struck an iceberg, sir."
25 "What avoiding action did you take?"

"I gave the order for 'Stop engines!' Then 'Full speed astern'."

"And the helm order?"

---

3 **to cast light** to shine – 4 **mate** person one works with, friend – 4 **to feel** confident to be sure –
4 **to recognize sth** to see sth and know what it is – 7 **to spring** *here:* to move as quickly as possible –
10 **desperately** ['despərətli] with great fear – 11 **to rush** *here:* to come, approach very quickly – 13 **port** left side of a ship – 13 **vibration** [vaɪ'breɪʃən] – 14 **full speed astern / ahead** [ə'stɜːn / ə'hed] *volle Kraft zurück / voraus* – 18 **tearing (noise)** noise which cloth makes when torn or pulled into two pieces –
18 **grinding (noise)** noise which steel makes when torn by sth very hard – 19 **to strike** to hit hard –
27 **helm** wheel that controls the direction in which a ship travels

"'Hard a' starboard', sir. I had to wait a few seconds, because I couldn't see the berg. This berg was more black than white."

"What was our speed when we struck?"

"About 18 knots, sir."

"You've closed the watertight doors?"

"Of course, sir."

The Captain looked forward from the bridge. The whole deck was covered with ice that had been shaken off the iceberg by the shock of the collision.

By far the largest part of an iceberg is under water. Some icebergs have a huge shelf which sticks out just below the surface. They are as hard as rock and extremely sharp. They can crush and cut through the steel plates of a ship's hull as if it were a tin can.

This is what happened to the *Titanic*. A stoker described what it was like:

"All of a sudden," he said, "the starboard side of the ship came in on us. It burst like a big gun going off. The water came pouring in and washed round our legs."

He and his mate just got through into the next stokehold before the bulkhead closed.

The Captain looked at his watch. It was 11.43 p.m.

For centuries ships had been steered according to so-called "tiller orders". The tiller order "hard a' starboard" meant "turn left". This is because the tiller, a lever attached to the rudder, had to be moved to the right to make the ship turn to the left. Modern ships have steering wheels that have to be turned to the right to make them turn right. So, tiller orders have not been used on big ships since the 1930s.

---

1 **starboard** the right side of a ship – 8 **shock** *here:* crash, heavy blow – 11 **huge** [hjuːdʒ] very big indeed – 12 **extremely** very – 12 **to crush** to break sth into pieces with heavy blows – 13 **hull** ['hʌl] *Schiffsrumpf* – 14 **stoker** person who works putting coal on a fire – 17 **to burst** to explode – 17 **to go off (of guns)** to fire – 19 **stokehold** space in a ship where stokers work – 20 **bulkhead** ['bʌlkhed] *Schott (Trennwand in einem Schiff)*

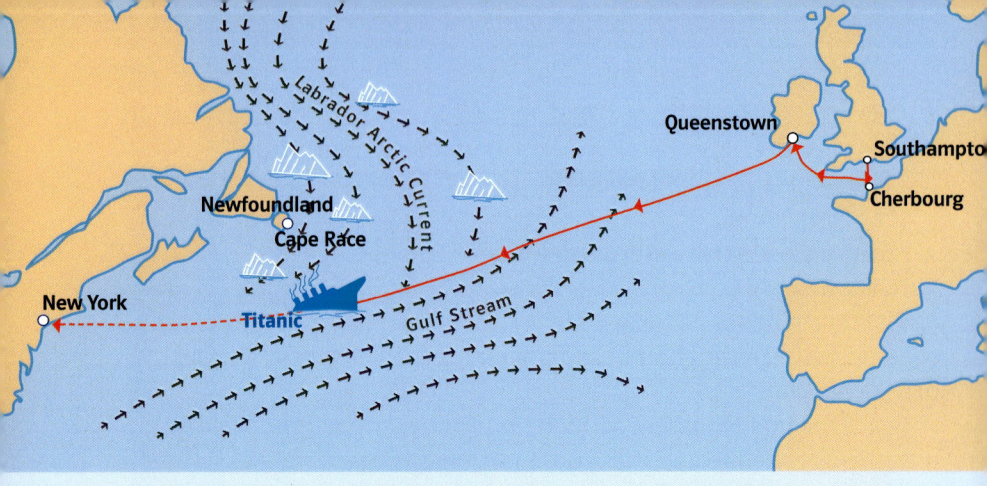

3 The Unbelievable News

Many of the passengers knew that something had happened. A Swiss girl, asleep in her cabin, woke up and asked, "Have we arrived?" She had the feeling the ship was scraping along a wall
5 the dockside. Lawrence Beesley felt the mattress on his bunk suddenly vibrate, quite gently, but enough to make him wonder. He also heard, coming up from below, a grinding noise, the noise that First Officer Murdoch had heard on the bridge. He went up on deck.

A steward sitting with his friends in the dining-saloon said that a
10 propeller had fallen off and they would have to go back to Belfast. He had known this happen before. It would mean some welcome leave! Both passengers and crew heard and felt the collision in different ways. Many on the top decks and in the staterooms did not hear it at all. One passenger remembered looking at his watch.
15 It was 11.45, he said.

"I was just getting into my bunk, when the ship seemed to roll, but so slightly that if I had had a glass in my hand filled to the top with water, not a drop would have spilled."

---

4 **to scrape** to rub against sth sharp or rough – 5 **mattress** ['mætrəs] soft part of the bed to lie on –
5 **bunk** narrow bed fixed to a wall – 10 **propeller** [prə'pelə] *Schiffsschraube* – 12 **leave** holiday, free
time for soldiers, seamen etc. – 13 **top deck** highest floor on a ship – 13 **stateroom** ['steɪtrʊm] first
class cabin for passengers – 17 **slightly** very little

Another passenger had left his porthole open and a shower of ice fell on to his floor. A man playing cards in an upper deck saloon also saw the iceberg and guessed there had been a collision. He joked about it, holding up his glass. Mr Beesley, who was passing, heard him say, "There must be plenty of ice somewhere on deck. Anyone be kind enough to go and get me some for my whisky?" His friends laughed.

At that moment the engines stopped, and the ship was suddenly still. One of the card-playing party said, "I expect the Captain has stopped to have the scratches repainted. What would the New Yorkers say if the *Titanic* arrived with a scratch down her side!"

The stopping of the engines caused the passengers little concern. Some of them put on coats over their night clothes and made their way up on deck. Lawrence Beesley, observing his fellow passengers, was surprised how calm they seemed. He realised that most of them had not come out on deck because they were alarmed, but because they were curious. They never thought for one moment that there was any real danger. They knew that the *Titanic* was unsinkable.

Two girls rushed by laughing. "I've never seen an iceberg!" one of them said. "Come on!"

They and a few other passengers saw the iceberg sail past and disappear into the darkness. It was an exciting experience, especially for the younger ones. Some of the older passengers asked the stewards why the *Titanic* had stopped, and the stewards answered, quite honestly, that they did not know. "Anyway, there's no need to worry. I'm sure it's nothing serious." They, like most of the crew, knew little about the accident, and they had the same complete faith in the ship as the passengers.

As the ship floated on the calm sea, men and women began to pick up pieces of ice from the deck to take home as souvenirs! Some even played football with a lump of ice, until the cold became too

---

1 **porthole** ['pɔːthəʊl] small round window on the side of a ship – 3 **to joke** *here:* to say sth funny –
10 **scratch** long mark made by sth sharp on ships, cars, tables etc. – 12 **concern** [kən'sɜːn] worry –
14 **to observe** to watch people / things to see how they behave – 15 **calm** *here:* not showing fear –
17 **curious** ['kjʊəriəs] *here:* wanting to understand what is happening – 22 **experience** *here:* something which happens – 25 **honest** ['ɒnɪst] *here:* true – 28 **faith** trust, believing in sb / sth –
30 **souvenir** [ˌsuːvən'ɪə] sth one keeps in memory of a holiday etc. – 31 **lump** large piece

much for them. Then they went into the saloons or returned to their cabins. A few even went back to bed.

Meanwhile third-class passengers and crew in the forward part of the ship had a very different experience, for they were on the lowest deck. The postal clerks in the lower mail room suddenly found water pouring in so fast that it was soon up to their knees. They lifted up the mail-bags and carried them up the iron staircase to the office above. But five minutes later, the office, too, began to flood. Astonishingly, the postal clerks saw no reason to worry. They retired to the deck above and, with two first-class passengers, watched the letters floating on the rising water.

"I'd like to know what's in those letters!" one of the clerks said.

"Well, they'll never get their love letters now!" said one of his mates.

The knowledge of those watertight compartments made them all feel safe.

Some of the third-class passengers whose cabins were on the starboard side forward heard the crash distinctly. The split in the hull was not far below them and the water was already rushing upwards. Carl Johnsson, lying in his bunk, heard a strange noise outside his door. He got up, and as he put on his socks, he saw water flowing into his cabin. It was quite clearly sea water. He dressed quickly, but the water soon covered his feet. Other third-class passengers had the same sort of experience as Johnsson. But they were not frightened, because, like everyone else, they believed the *Titanic* to be unsinkable. Picking up as much luggage as they could carry, for they did not want it to be spoiled by the salt water, they made their way to the third-class staircase.

Meanwhile one of the mail clerks decided to go and report to the Captain. He reached the bridge at the same time as the carpenter, who was out of breath.

"Water is pouring into the ship, sir, on the starboard side forward," the carpenter said.

"The mail rooms are flooded, sir," said the postal clerk.

---

5 **clerk** [klɑːk] clerks work in offices of all kinds – 5 **mail** letters – 8 **to flood** [flʌd] to fill or cover with water – 9 **to retire** *here:* to move away from ... and up to – 27 **to spoil** to damage seriously

The Captain, who had just sent one of his junior officers forward to look for damage, was thunderstruck. The junior officer had reported no damage! The Captain decided to send for Thomas Andrews immediately.

5 Bruce Ismay had felt and heard the crash. He was out of bed in a second. He pulled on a pair of trousers over his pyjamas, put on a coat and hurried to the bridge. He wanted desperately to know what had happened. The news alarmed him.

"Andrews will be here any minute," the Captain told Ismay. "He's 10 the only one of us who will know for certain how serious the damage is."

Andrews was in his stateroom studying plans of the *Titanic*, and noting down the changes he wanted to make. His mind was so occupied that he had neither heard nor felt the crash. But when 15 called, he went straight to the bridge, and then, with the Captain, climbed down to the lowest decks forward to find out what had happened.

After only ten minutes below, Andrews turned to the Captain.

"The ship is sinking," he said. "Nothing can save her now."

20 The Captain was speechless.

"If only two of the watertight compartments were flooded," Andrews went on, "there would be no problem. If four were flooded she'd probably stay afloat. But at the moment the fifth compartment is filling up. The bulkhead between the fifth and sixth compartments 25 is not high enough to keep the water out. Before long the water from the fifth compartment will spill over into the sixth compartment. The iceberg has cut through the plates to about a third of the length of the ship."

"How long will she stay afloat?" Captain Smith asked.

30 "About two and a half hours," Andrews said calmly.

The Captain looked at his watch. It was just after midnight.

2 **thunderstruck** terribly surprised – 13 **to note down** to write notes about – 13 **his mind was so occupied** his thoughts were so full of … – 20 **speechless** unable to speak – 25 **to keep out** to stop (the water) from entering – 26 **to spill over** to start flowing over the top of

19

The Russian East Asiatic S.S. Co.   Radio-Telegram.

M16307

S.S. "Birma".

Words.	Origin.Station.	Time handed in.	Via.	Remarks.
g to	Titanic	11 H.45M.April 14/15 1912.		Distress ca Ligs Loud

Cgd - Sos. from M. G. Y.

　　We have struck iceberg sinking fast come to our assis
tance.

　　Position Lat. 41.46 n. Lon. 50.14. w.

　　　　　M.G.Y.

4 S.O.S.!

　　Marconi's invention, wireless, was one of the wonders of
the early twentieth century. In 1912 many ships still did not have
wireless operators, and those that did, rarely had more than one
5　operator. The *Titanic* had two, George Phillips, the senior, Harold
Bride, the junior. These two young men and their wireless played a
life and death role in the drama of the *Titanic*.

　　On the evening of April 14th the passengers on the *Titanic*
regarded the ship's wireless as an exciting new plaything, for their
10　amusement. The *Titanic* was now near enough to the wireless station
on Cape Race, Newfoundland, to receive and send messages. So

2 **Marconi's invention** radio, wireless – 7 **role** part (usually in the theatre)

20

first and second-class passengers thought it would be fun to send telegrams to their relatives and friends. First operator Phillips was kept so busy tapping out these quite unimportant messages that he neglected the most urgent ice warning the *Titanic* had yet received. At 9.40 the *S.S. Mesaba* had sent the following message:

> *To Titanic and all west-bound ships … saw much heavy pack-ice and a great number of icebergs.*

The position which the *Mesaba* gave lay right across the *Titanic's* path. Yet the overworked Phillips put it on one side and forgot about it. The *Titanic* was still steaming at 22 knots and was holding her course. It is impossible to know how fatal Phillips' mistake was. It is impossible to know whether Captain Smith would have altered course or slowed down, if he had read the message. But no one blames Phillips for the disaster. He had received so many ice warnings and nothing had been done.

Phillips and the second wireless operator, Bride, were friends. Bride felt that Phillips had overworked and so offered to relieve him at midnight instead of at the usual time, 2.00 a.m. At 11.55 Bride came along to the wireless cabin and asked how things were going. Phillips told him that he had heard the ship was damaged and that it was probably going back to Belfast for repairs. Bride dressed, came back and put on the headphones. At that moment the Captain entered the cabin.

"We've struck an iceberg and I'm having an inspection made to find out what it has done to us. You'd better get ready to send out a call for assistance, but don't send it until I tell you."

Phillips took the headphones from Bride and put them back on again. In less than a quarter of an hour the Captain was back. "Send the call for assistance," he said, handing Phillips a piece of paper which gave the ship's position but no details of damage.

---

3 **to tap** to hit gently with the finger. *Here* he is tapping a message in Morse Code. – 4 **urgent** ['ɜːdʒənt] sth which must be dealt with very quickly – 9 **overworked** made to work too hard – 11 **fatal** [feɪtəl] causing death or a catastrophe – 14 **to blame sb** to say that sb has done sth wrong – 17 **to relieve** *here*: to take sb's place – 22 **headphones** ['hedfəʊnz] *Kopfhörer* – 26 **assistance** help

Phillips and Bride laughed at the Captain's order. The ship had stopped, which was unusual, but they, like everyone else, believed the *Titanic* to be unsinkable. Naturally Phillips tapped out the distress signal, CQD (Come quickly! Danger!) and gave the *Titanic's* position. He tapped the signal again and again.

"Why don't you send the new signal for a change – S.O.S. (Save our Souls)?" Bride said with a grin.

Phillips smiled. "All right!" he said, and he began to tap out S.O.S. It was the first time this famous cry for help had ever been used at sea. All the ships that had so far received the *Titanic's* call for help were too far away. The *Olympic* was 500 miles away. The German ship, *Frankfort*, was 150 miles away, but by an extraordinary piece of luck Phillips reached the *Carpathia*, a small Cunard liner, which was only 58 miles away. The *Carpathia*, like all small ships, only carried one wireless operator. Harold Cottam had just gone out on deck, having finished his watch. Then, before going below, he decided to return to the wireless cabin and call the *Titanic* on some quite unimportant matter. He and Phillips knew each other. No sooner had he put on the headphones than he heard Phillips' urgent distress signal: 'CQD! CQD! S.O.S.!' He could not believe it!

Cottam took down the *Titanic's* position, astonished.

"Do you want me to inform the Captain?" he asked.

"Yes! Yes!" Phillips replied. "Come quickly!"

Cottam took the *Titanic's* distress signal up to the bridge. Then he and the First Officer burst into the Captain's cabin and told him the news. The *Carpathia* had been moving carefully through the ice, but now the Captain gave the order for full steam ahead and raced through the darkness and the ice to the *Titanic's* assistance.

Arthur Rostron, Captain of the *Carpathia*, was a courageous and efficient officer, as well as a first-class navigator. He was making for the Mediterranean, but now gave the order to turn north. He soon reached the icebergs, but steered skilfully between them without reducing speed. He had already ordered the doctor and the chief

---

4 **distress signal** [dɪsˈtresˌsɪɡnəl] signal sent out calling for immediate help – 18 **matter** subject – 29 **courageous** [kəˈreɪdʒəs] brave – 30 **efficient** [ɪˈfɪʃənt] good at his work – 30 **to make for** to go in the direction of – 32 **skilfully** very efficiently

steward to be completely prepared for survivors. Spaces in the saloon were cleared and blankets brought out. Food and hot drinks were prepared, and even the lifeboats were swung out in readiness. Captain Rostron expected to have to take on board 3,000 people. The Chief Steward gave a little talk to his staff, which he finished thus: "Let every man do his duty like a true Englishman. If the situation calls for it, let us add another glorious page to British history."

Meanwhile Harold Cottam tapped out messages to Phillips and waited anxiously for his reply. It was getting colder and colder, but Cottam did not even put on his jacket. He was too busy to notice the cold. Here is an extract from his log:

Sunday, April 14th, 1912

11.20 p.m.   *Heard Titanic calling S.O.S. and CQD. Answered him immediately. Titanic says 'struck iceberg. Come to our assistance at once. Position 41° 46' N; long. 50° 14' E.' Informed bridge at once.*

11.30 p.m.   *Course altered; proceeding to the scene of the disaster.*

11.45 p.m.   *Titanic says weather calm and clear. Engine-room is getting flooded.*

Monday, April 15th, 1912

12.10 a.m.   *Titanic calling CQD. His power seems greatly reduced.*

12.20 a.m   *Titanic's signals very broken.*

12.25 a.m.   *Called Titanic. No response.*

12.30 a.m.   *Continued to call Titanic at frequent intervals, but no response.*

Note the hour's difference in time between *Titanic* and *Carpathia*. The *Carpathia* was about sixty miles west of the *Titanic*.

1 **survivor** [sə'vaɪvə] sb who is still alive after a catastrophe – 1 **space** empty place – 3 **lifeboat** a boat kept on a ship for people to use when the ship is sinking – 3 **in readiness** *here:* ready to be lowered if necessary – 5 **staff** persons who work under managers, headteachers, businessmen etc. – 11 **extract** short passage from a book, newspaper etc. – 17 **to proceed** to go – 18 **disaster** catastrophe – 22 **power** *here:* strength – 22 **to reduce** to become less – 25 **response** [rɪ'spɒns] reply – 26 **at frequent intervals** ['ɪntəvəlz] with only short pauses

There was another ship, the *Californian*, much closer to the *Titanic* than the *Carpathia*. The *Californian* was not one of the smartest British liners. She was, in fact, the sort of ship the fashionable set would have been ashamed to sail in. Her lights
5 could be clearly seen from the *Titanic's* decks and she seemed not to be moving. The distance between the two ships was estimated at between eight and ten miles. Earlier in the day the *Californian's* wireless operator, Evans, had tried to warn Phillips of the ice. But Phillips, who was desperately busy with his telegrams, had told him
10 crossly not to interrupt. Evans went off duty at 11.50, and the Third Officer took his place. This young man, however, though extremely interested in wireless telegraphy, still understood very little about it. He put on the headphones and then pressed different switches – with no success. He heard nothing. If by some lucky chance he had
15 pressed the right switches, he would have heard Phillips' distress signals. The *Californian* could have found a way through the ice and reached the *Titanic* at least an hour before she went down.

---

3 **smart** fashionable – 6 **distance** how far it is between two places – 10 **cross** angry – 10 **to interrupt** [ˌɪntəˈrʌpt] to break in on sb who is speaking, working – 10 **to go off duty** to stop work

5 All Passengers on Deck!

When the Captain gave the order, 'Everyone on deck with lifebelts!' most people obeyed, but slowly and without any sense of urgency. Some did not wake up and were allowed to go on sleeping by their partners. Many, especially those in Third Class, never got the message. There was no public announcement system in those days, no loud-speakers. If the Captain wanted to talk to the passengers, he had to shout into a megaphone or make use of his stewards and officers as messengers.

---

3 **sense** *here:* feeling – 5 **partner** *here:* husband or wife – 6 **public announcement** system talking to many people at the same time in a ship, building etc., using a microphone and many loudspeakers

At 12.05 a.m. stewards began moving from stateroom to stateroom, cabin to cabin, knocking politely. Even at a moment like this, first-class passengers must be treated with respect, and if they needed attention, attention must be given them. There had been no lifeboat drill and some of the passengers did not know how to put on their lifebelts. Stewards stopped to help them. One steward even helped the multi-millionaire, Guggenheim, to dress. Few of the stewards felt any sense of urgency. They, too, believed in that well-worn phrase, 'The *Titanic* is unsinkable'.

Some passengers refused to move because they were convinced there was no danger. William Stead, whose steward had to help him into his lifebelt, complained that it was all quite unnecessary. Guggenheim took his lifebelt off after his steward had spent several minutes fixing it on him. "It hurts!" he said. So the steward put it on for him again. Another steward had a problem with a locked door. He knocked loudly, but there was no answer. He could hear through the door a man and a woman talking in a low voice. They refused to come out even when he told them the ship had hit an iceberg. The multi-millionaire, Jacob Astor and his wife, went to the gymnasium and sat on the vaulting horses.

Second-class stewards were less polite in dealing with their passengers. Instead of knocking, they just threw open the doors and shouted, "Everyone on deck with lifebelts!" As for the third-class passengers, the stewards neglected them. They were left to look after themselves in the most dangerous part of the ship near, and soon below, the waterline. Those who had their cabins forward did not need any warning. The sight of the rising water was enough. Many of them ran along the long passage which connected the third-class sleeping quarters forward with the sleeping quarters aft. They brought the news that the *Titanic* had struck an iceberg and that their cabins were already filling up with water. They did not panic. They were not even frightened. How could they feel any

---

4 **attention** *here:* looking after – 5 **(life)boat drill** *Rettungsübung* – 10 **to refuse** [rɪ'fjuːz] to say no – 10 **convinced** completely certain – 12 **to complain** to protest – 17 **low voice** opposite of loud – 20 **vaulting horse** apparatus for jumping in a gymnasium – 24 **to neglect** to forget about, do nothing for sb – 27 **sight** what can be seen – 27 **to rise** to go up – 29 **quarters** *here:* where third class have their cabins and rooms

anxiety in such a huge ship as the *Titanic*? She might have been holed by an iceberg, but she would not sink.

Passengers brought with them on to the boat deck the strangest objects. First-class passenger, Edith Russell, had with her a musical
5 pig that she was especially fond of because she had bought it during her stay in Paris. She had packed her trunks very carefully and had locked them up. As she was leaving her cabin, she said to her steward,

"Take these keys and mail them to me as soon as the ship reaches
10 Halifax."

There was a strange rumour on board, and on shore, that the passengers were going to be taken off in the lifeboats, while the *Titanic* sailed on to Halifax, Canada, with her crew. The steward, who was one of the few who guessed how serious the situation was,
15 replied:

"You go and kiss your trunks goodbye! I've got five children at home and I'm worried."

But he did go back and get her musical pig.

Lawrence Beesley filled his coat pockets with books. Stewart
20 Collett, another second-class passenger, took with him a Bible which he had promised his brother he would always carry with him until their next meeting. Third-class passenger, Adolf Dyker, gave his wife, Elizabeth, a little bag in which there were two gold watches, some valuable jewellery and 200 Swedish crowns. A first-
25 class Canadian passenger, Colonel Peuchen, left behind documents worth 300,000 dollars and picked up instead a good-luck pin and three oranges.

Many of the ladies had left their jewellery with the ship's Purser. Now they wanted it back. But the Purser refused to waste time
30 dealing with their requests. He was down below on C deck at the foot of the great staircase, hurrying people along.

---

4 **object** ['ɒbdʒɪkt] thing – 5 **to be fond of** to like very much – 9 **to mail** to post letters – 10 **Halifax** port in Nova Scotia, Canada – 14 **to guess** [gɛs] *here:* to feel sure one knows – without knowing the facts – 24 **valuable** ['væljuəbl] worth a lot of money – 24 **crown** *here:* a Swedish coin (money) – 25 **documents** important papers – 26 **pin** sharp, thin piece of metal used for fixing pieces of cloth together – 28 **purser** ['pɜːsə] officer who keeps passengers' money or jwellery in a ships safe *(Zahlmeister)* – 29 **to waste time** to spend time doing unimportant things – 30 **request** sth one asks for – 31 **to hurry people along** to tell people to hurry

"Hurry, little lady!" he said to the Countess of Rothes as she passed him on her way to the deck. "Thank you for not asking me for your jewels!"

Henry Sleeper Harper, director of a famous American publishing firm, had brought on deck his prize-winning Peke, Sun-Yat-Sen, while a girl was carrying a Pomeranian. "We'd better find a lifebelt for the doggie!" a man joked. Miss Edith Russell's musical pig undoubtedly saved her life. She refused to move when ordered into the lifeboat – until some understanding person pulled the pig out of her hands and threw it into the boat. Miss Russell immediately jumped after it.

There was so little fear and anxiety that the crew had no difficulty in keeping each class to its own deck. This meant that the first-class passengers had a great advantage over the other two classes, especially the third-class, who were still deep down in the ship near the waterline. At that moment the emigrants might not have envied the great ladies and gentlemen of the First Class, for it was freezing cold on the upper decks. There was no wind, the sea was calm and the stars shone brightly, but there was ice floating on the dark water and the temperature had sunk to 28 °F (-3.5 °C).

Some women still had on their nightdresses covered only by a blanket or a shawl. Some of the wealthiest passengers were dressed as if they were going to a ball. The women wore their long skirts and top-heavy party hats. The men wore black ties and tailor-made dinner jackets, or else fashionable suits with smart capes.

At 12.05 the Captain had given the order, 'Prepare the lifeboats!'. It was now nearly 12.30. The boats were ready. The covers had been removed and each boat was provided with tins of biscuits and an oil lamp. It had taken longer than the crew had expected, for they had had great difficulty in swinging the boats out over the side. The machinery was new and stiff, and even the officers did not completely understand how it worked. Neither passengers nor crew

---

5 **Peke, Pomeranian** [ˌpɒməˈreɪnɪən] small dogs – 14 **to have an advantage over** *here:* to have a better chance than – 16 **to envy** [ˈenvi] to want sth sb else has – 22 **shawl** worn round a woman's shoulders, usually made of wool – 22 **wealthy** [ˈwelθi] rich – 23 **ball** *here:* a dance in fashionable society – 24 **tailor-made** made especially for a customer by a tailor – 25 **cape** coat without sleeves, hangs round shoulders – 31 **stiff** moving with difficulty

had ever had any boat drill. The men worked so hard they sweated, despite the cold.

> The *Titanic* had 16 wooden lifeboats, eight on the port side and eight on the starboard side. She also had four canvas collapsible lifeboats. When fully loaded these 20 boats could carry 1,178 people. No passengers, and only a few members of the crew, knew that there was not nearly enough lifeboat space for the 2,207 people on board. The wooden lifeboats were numbered 1 to 16, the collapsibles, A to D.

The passengers, on the other hand, stood shivering, waiting patiently to be told what to do. Very few of them knew the truth. Even the officers did not know that already the *Titanic* was sinking fast. The Captain kept his terrible secret to himself, still afraid of panic. As for Thomas Andrews, he only told the truth to those he could completely trust. He thought it was too early to spread alarm and destroy people's confidence in the 'world's safest liner'. Mrs Caldwell, a second-class passenger, remembered asking a sailor, as she climbed on board at Southampton, if the *Titanic* was really unsinkable. "Unsinkable, lady?" the sailor replied. "God himself couldn't sink the Titanic!"

And that is what nearly everyone thought, as the first lifeboats were swung out. Some people were worried by the deafening roar of steam escaping from a pipe in one of the funnels. It did not seem natural. But they felt much safer here, on the solid decks of the giant ship, than in 'those little wooden boats'.

But how would they have felt if they had known that the first four watertight compartments were already flooded ten minutes after

---

1 **to sweat** [swet] to become wet as a result of hard work – 4 **collapsible (boat)** [kə'læpsəbl] a lifeboat that can be folded, so it can be stored in a smaller place – 10 **to shiver** to shake with cold or fear – 11 **patiently** ['peɪʃəntli] *here:* calmly, quietly – 13 **secret** sth which only a few people know – 22 **deafening** very loud indeed – 22 **roar** [rɔː] loud and frightening noise – 23 **pipe** *here:* water, oil, steam etc. pass through long pipes – 24 **solid** thick and strong

the collision? Would there have been panic if they had learned that there was room in the lifeboats for only half the people on board, including the crew? These are important questions, because if there had been more urgency, more people might have been saved.

5   There were few laws in those days about safety measures at sea, and in this respect the *Titanic* was no worse than any other ship.

---

5 **law ... safety measures** Governments in those days had done little to force shipping companies to make their ships safe at sea. – 6 **in this respect** concerning this subject, question

6 Women and Children First!

At 12.30 the Captain gave the order, 'All men stand back. All women and children to the deck below'. It was thought that from the lower deck women would be able to step more easily into the life-
5 boats. But the magic of the *Titanic* was too strong for many of them. The lights were still blazing. The band was playing ragtime nearby, and many of the married women refused to leave their husbands.

5 **magic** ['mædʒɪk] *here:* their almost superstitious confidence in the Titanic – 6 **to blaze** *here:* to shine brightly – 6 **ragtime** popular kind of music invented by American blacks

Wrecks suggested storms and great waves. How could a great ship like the *Titanic* sink in a sea as smooth as glass? So the first lifeboat, No. 7, went down with only twenty people in it. It had room for six-ty-six. The Captain's order, 'Women and children first!' meant that husbands were not allowed to go with their wives, even if there was room. Very few husbands would have agreed anyway, because the tradition of 'behaving like a gentleman' was too strong, both among the Americans and the British. So millionaires, distinguished men of all kinds, gave way to stewardesses and to women from the Third Class, when at last these unfortunate people were allowed on to the boat deck. Many of them helped the crew to load the boats.

Annie Martin from Portsmouth and another stewardess were standing back from the boats when Bruce Ismay came up to them and told them to get in.

"Oh, we can't, sir," Annie said. "We're members of the crew."

"You're women, too, aren't you? Go on! Get into the boat! "

They obeyed. Annie remembered seeing a man force his way into one of the boats, waving a gun and saying that he would shoot anyone who tried to stop him. Annie also said that two other men forced their way into her boat, and were not pulled out.

Meanwhile, Bruce Ismay was rushing from boat to boat in a state of hysteria. He shouted again and again, "Women and children first!" He was anxious to help, but became such a nuisance that Fifth Officer Lowe lost his temper with him. Bruce Ismay retired at once, and took no more part in the operation. He was already a broken man.

Violet Jessop, a pretty and observant stewardess, felt there was a lack of control, and that the organisation was not as good as it should have been. On her way to the deck she noticed bell boys and lift-boys laughing and smoking and rushing about the first-class saloon, thoroughly enjoying themselves. They were all in their early teens and should have been waiting their turn on the lifeboat

---

1 **wreck** [rek] ship that has sunk or run on the rocks – 7 **tradition** old custom or habit which still lives – 9 **to give way** to let other people go first – 17 **to force one's way** to get somewhere by pushing other people out of the way – 23 **nuisance** ['njuːsəns] sth/sb that causes trouble – 24 **to lose one's temper** to get angry suddenly – 25 **operation** *here:* action – 27 **observant** noticing things – 28 **lack of** not enough

deck. Nobody bothered about them. Second Officer Lightoller would certainly have refused them a place in the boats. He would even have kept out the thirteen-year-old son of millionaire Arthur Ryerson, if the father had not insisted. Is a boy of thirteen a child or a man? Today there would be no need to ask, but in 1912, he was considered a young man.

On the stairs, Violet Jessop passed two boys pulling up with great effort a heavy bag, which suddenly burst open. Golden sovereigns spilled out of it. Violet imagined that the boys had broken into the Purser's office. Nobody stopped to pick the coins up as they rolled down the stairs. She passed the Captain and Thomas Andrews talking together in a low voice and wondered what they were discussing. She liked Thomas Andrews. All the crew did, especially the stewardesses. He was always kind and helpful and gave good advice on how to treat the passengers. Since the collision he had moved about the ship, telling everyone in a calm voice that they must hurry to the boat deck, that it was urgent. Yet he always managed to prevent people from panicking.

Once on the boat deck Violet found a baby left behind by its mother. She picked it up and wrapped it in the eiderdown she had brought with her, and when her turn came to get into the boat, she took the baby with her.

Mr and Mrs Harder, who were one of thirteen honeymoon couples on board, were especially lucky. As soon as they heard the call, 'All passengers on deck!', they went up to the uncovered lifeboats and jumped into one of them, 'just for fun'. "We never thought the boat would have to be used, so we just stayed there. Nobody turned us out, not even when the Captain ordered 'Women and children only'."

Second Officer Lightoller, in charge of the boats on the port side, was extremely strict where men were concerned. He would not allow any men passengers in the boats at all. Men had a much better

1 **to bother** about to take notice of – 4 **to insist** to say that sth must be done – 8 **effort** trying hard –
8 **sovereign** ['sɒvrɪn] golden coin worth £1 – 20 **to wrap** [ræp] to cover, put sth round sb, sth –
20 **eiderdown** ['aɪdədaʊn] thick, soft covering for a bed – 23 **honeymoon** ['hʌnimuːn] first holiday of
a married couple

chance on the starboard side, where First Officer Murdoch was in charge. Murdoch allowed men to fill up empty spaces. Yet some men still stood back, not wishing to appear cowardly or unmanly. The elderly Dr Washington Dodge had to be pushed into a lifeboat by a friendly steward.

Murdoch lowered lifeboat No. 1 with only twelve people in it. It contained Sir Cosmo Duff Gordon, Lady Duff Gordon and her maid, two Americans, and six stokers that Murdoch had added, because he was unable to find any more passengers. He had put lookout Symons in charge. It was 12.45, and no third-class passengers had appeared yet on the boat deck.

While the first-class passengers were stepping unwillingly into the boats, two stewards stood at the top of the Third Class staircase and kept the hundreds of emigrants below decks. They were crowded around the bottom of the stairs and all along the narrow passage leading aft. There was complete confusion. Hundreds of them could not speak English, and were unable to put on their lifebelts without help from the stewards.

Many had brought all their luggage with them, which added to the confusion. They were so far down in the ship that few of them could ever have found their way through the labyrinth of passages to the boat deck. Some did get there – by pushing aside barriers and stewards – and most of these enterprising people found a place in a boat. As for the rest, they had to wait and they became noisier and noisier. There was no panic, because they, too, believed that the *Titanic* could not sink, but they wanted to know what was going on, and no one would tell them.

At last the steward, Hart, took a party of women and children up to the boat deck and came back for another. He set out with his second and last party at 1.30. He could not return for a third, because Murdoch ordered him to get into the boat himself.

The third-class passengers were now entirely on their own. No member of the crew came to help them. They found that many

3 **cowardly** ['kaʊədli] opposite of brave – 3 **unmanly** a man ought not to show fear – 12 **unwillingly** not wanting to – 16 **confusion** there is confusion when no one knows what is happening or what to do – 21 **labyrinth** ['læbərɪnθ] – 23 **enterprising** having the courage and willingness to do sth difficult – 32 **entirely** completely

of the doors between Third Class and the other classes were still locked, and gradually as the ship tilted they began to realise that the *Titanic* was sinking after all.

2 **to tilt** to move downwards, to slope

7 Away Lifeboats!

By 12.45 the Captain was getting desperate. The *Californian*, whose lights everybody could still see so clearly, had not moved. A signal flashed in Morse got no answer. So the Captain fired his
5 first distress rocket, and went on firing them at intervals until 1.40 a.m. The rockets disturbed people more than anything else. They thought: 'If the Captain thinks rockets are necessary, then we must be in danger'. Besides, the deck was tilting more and more towards the bows.

10 Husbands began to force their wives to get into the lifeboats. Some women were torn from their husbands and carried kicking and screaming to the boats. An emigrant, Mrs Yasbeck, did not

4 **to flash** *here:* to send a signal in Morse Code using a special lamp – 4 **Morse (code)** [ˌmɔːsˈkəʊd] a set of long and short sounds (or flashes of light) representing numbers and the alphabet – 5 **at intervals** *here:* every seven minutes – 12 **to scream** to shout with fear, pain or anger

realise until too late that her husband was not in the boat with her. As the boat was being lowered she screamed that she wanted to go back on board. No one could persuade second-class passenger, Mrs Charlotte Collyer, to leave her husband. Two seamen had to pull her away, sobbing and screaming.

"Be brave, Charlotte," her husband called. "I'll find a place in another boat."

The arrival of the first group of third-class passengers added to the confusion. There was no panic, but the Captain was afraid there might be. So he ordered the officers to arm themselves with guns. They did not need them. Some men did jump into the boats, but they were pulled out again without a struggle. One young boy, who was discovered hiding under a seat, just argued when the officer threatened him with his gun, but climbed out when he was told to 'behave like a man'. A young Irish emigrant, Daniel Buckley, managed to get a place in a boat by putting a shawl over his head. Some say that Mrs Astor, the millionaire's wife, covered him with it.

To the very end Lightoller refused to allow any men except crew members into his boats. He was an officer whom people obeyed because he was a man to be respected and admired. It is true there were still plenty of women on board. But most of them were from the Third Class and were wandering about the lower decks hopelessly lost, and beginning to feel desperate. Yet no one was sent to find them and the last two boats were lowered half empty. There was little time left, for the ship's head was already under water and there was now only five metres between the boat deck and the sea. Two enterprising young men, Hugh Woolner and a Norwegian, Bjornstrom Steffanson, walked down the sloping deck and jumped into the boat just as it reached the water.

The ship was tilting more and more. The bows had now disappeared completely and most of the forward deck, too. Everyone left on the *Titanic*, emigrants, third-class women who had at last found their way to the open deck, the boys whom Violet Jessop had seen playing in the first-class saloon, all made a rush

---

5 **to sob** to cry when one is in deep distress – 12 **struggle** [strʌgl] fight – 13 **to argue** to refuse to listen or do what one is told

for the stern and crowded there together. They understood at last that the *Titanic* was not unsinkable. They realised with horror that all along the officers had known there was no place for them in the lifeboats, and the terrible truth struck them that they had almost certainly kissed their wives and children goodbye for the last time. Most of them did not expect to survive. Some of them knew so little about the sea that they did not know the awful fate that lay in store for them.

The ship suddenly rolled to port. They were swept off their feet and fell in a heap against the railings. They struggled to their feet and hung on to anything they could find, as the stern rose higher and higher out of the water.

Meanwhile the band continued to play ragtime, the Captain remained on the bridge and Phillips and Bride left the wireless room for the last time. It was now 2 o'clock. The lights were still on, thanks to a heroic group of stokers who kept one of the fires going until the last moment.

The bandmaster raised his hand and his players stopped. Then at a word from their chief, they began playing again. But this time it was not ragtime. They knew that the end had come. The music floated out across the sea in the clear, still night and was heard by the survivors in the lifeboats.

It will never be known for certain what that last tune was. Some say that it was a hymn, but other survivors swear that it was 'Nearer my God to Thee', while the wireless operator, Bride, is equally sure it was 'Autumn', a favourite slow waltz tune at that time. Whichever tune it was, it tragically suited the situation. The bandsmen made no effort to save themselves. Finally the deck slipped from under their feet and they were swallowed up by the icy waters.

The Captain stayed on the bridge until the sea washed him off. Some say they saw him in the water after the ship went down, with a baby in his arms. He handed the baby to somebody in a boat, then

1 **stern** [stɜːn] back part of a ship – 2 **horror** ['hɒrə] an awful surprise or fear – 3 **all along** all the time, from the beginning – 7 **their fate** what was going to happen to them – 7 **to lie in store** to be coming in the future – 10 **railing** ['reɪlɪŋ] kind of fence to protect people from falling off a ship –
11 **to hang on to** to hold tightly – 16 **heroic** [hɪˈrəʊɪk] very brave – 16 **to keep going** *here:* to keep the fires alight – 24 **hymn** [hɪm] a song of praise that Christians sing to God – 27 **to suit the situation** it was well chosen for the disaster which was to come

took off his lifebelt and sank out of sight. In any case, he did not want to live. It has even been claimed he shot himself.

Meanwhile, Bruce Ismay, managing director of the White Star Line, was sitting in one of the lifeboats, head bent, talking and listening to no one. It is not known for certain how he got into the lifeboat. Those who wish to excuse him say that he was told to go. His critics claim that he jumped into one of the last lifeboats just as it was about to be lowered. It would have been better if he had gone down with the ship, because he became one of the *Titanic's* living dead. He never recovered from the tragedy, and from then on shut himself away even from his own family.

The saddest and bravest man of all, Thomas Andrews, was last seen in a saloon, standing all alone and staring ahead of him. He had retired there when there was nothing more he could do to help the passengers. At last he could be alone with his tragic thoughts. Was it his fault that the 'safest ship in the world' was now sinking fast? No doubt he blamed himself. 'If I had given the ship a double skin ... ! If I had raised the bulkheads a few more feet ... ! If ...'

4 **head bent** head on his chest – 9 **living dead** he was not part of society any more – 17 **double skin** another hull inside the main hull

8 Every Man for Himself!

When the last lifeboat was safely launched, the Captain gave the order, 'Every man for himself!'. But Second Officer Lightoller was determined to try and save some of the unfortunate people still
5 left on board.

Of the *Titanic's* four collapsible boats, boats C and D had already been launched, but the other two, A and B, still lay collapsed on the deck. So Lightoller and others of the crew worked desperately to make them seaworthy. It was too late, for the *Titanic* was sinking
10 fast. Collapsible A was washed over the side half full of water, and Collapsible B launched itself upside down. But the two boats stayed afloat and Wireless Operator Bride, who was washed overboard at the same time, found himself *underneath* Collapsible B.

2 **to launch** ['lɔːntʃ] *here:* to put into the water – 4 **determined** very enterprising and ready to try hard – 9 **seaworthy** able to carry people without sinking – 10 **to wash** *here:* the rushing water carried (washed) the boat into the sea – 11 **upside down** bottom upwards

As the ship tilted more steeply, Lightoller and the others climbed aft towards the stern, now high out of the water. Suddenly their way was blocked by a crowd of third-class passengers struggling up to the deck from below. Among them were many women and children. Lightoller was filled with horror. He thought that all the women and children had got away safely in the lifeboats. The decks were now sloping so steeply that the weaker ones could hold on no longer. They began to fall and roll into the ice-filled sea. Lightoller knew there was nothing more he could do. He jumped and the water closed over him. He felt as if 'a thousand knives' had been driven into his body. He had never known such bitter cold …

Charles Joughin, Chief Baker, worked until the last possible moment taking loaves of bread to the lifeboats. Only when the last lifeboat had left did he think of saving himself. He remained quite calm. First he went below to his cabin and found it already under water. He sat on his bunk, opened his whisky bottle and swallowed enough to give him warmth against the cold. Then he climbed to the deck. He was only just in time, because a few minutes later the stairs would have been too steep. Joughin held on to the railings as men and women all round him were thrown into the sea. And as the ship suddenly twisted to port, he climbed over the railings, and holding tightly on to them, walked up the side of the ship. By the time he reached the stern, the *Titanic* was standing on her head, her nose deep in the ocean. Joughin stood on the rounded steel plates of the stern, which towered above the water. Almost at once there was a thunderous roar beneath his feet. The inner parts of the *Titanic* had broken loose and were crashing down the length of the ship.

Joughin stood firm, still quite confident that he would survive. For five minutes the ship hung there in the water, not moving. Then gradually she began to sink. "It was like going down in a lift," Joughin said, and he stepped into the water without even getting his head wet …

2 **to block the way** to stop sb from passing − 10 **to close over** to cover completely − 10 **to drive** *here:* to push hard − 16 **to swallow** ['swɒləʊ] to drink quickly − 21 **to twist** *here:* to turn sharply − 22 **tightly** *here:* with all one's strength − 24 **rounded** curved − 25 **to tower** to rise high above − 26 **inner parts** parts inside the ship − 27 **length** *here:* from one end of the ship to the other − 31 **gradually** slowly, little by little

Meanwhile the sixteen lifeboats and two collapsibles were rowing away from the *Titanic*, afraid of being sucked down with her when she finally disappeared. She was sinking fast, but the lights still shone brightly. At last, as the ship tilted steeply, the lights went out, came on again for a second, and then went out for ever. Then came the roar which Chief Baker Joughin heard, standing on the stern, and which some people thought were explosions.

The shivering people in the open boats watched tiny black figures falling from the stern. There was a moment's silence as they hit the icy water. The shock of the cold took their breath away. Then from all over the dark water there came cries for help. Some of the women who had left their sons or husbands behind begged the seamen in charge of their boats to go back and pick up the people struggling in the water. Other women begged the sailors not to listen. Their boats would only be upset by desperate men trying to climb on board. That was the opinion of most of the seamen. One boat was able to pull eight frozen men out of the water, because it was near enough for men to swim to. Other swimmers, desperately trying to reach a boat, actually saw it move away from them. Only Fifth Officer Lowe, in lifeboat No. 14, went back. But he, too, waited, afraid that the mass of people struggling in the water might overturn the boat. He waited too long, not realising how quickly the freezing water could kill. The desperate screams for help had now become a murmur. Fifth-Officer Lowe picked up only one woman and three men, one of whom died later in the boat. It was nearly an hour after the *Titanic* had gone down.

In Sir Cosmo Duff Gordon's lifeboat, which held only twelve people, a stoker said it was their duty to turn back and pick up survivors, but Sir Cosmo declared it would be too great a risk.

"We would be swamped," he said.

As Lightoller swam away from the sinking *Titanic*, he suddenly felt himself being pulled downwards. He thought his lungs were going to

---

1 **to row** [rəʊ] *rudern* – 2 **to suck down** to pull down (under the water) – 8 **tiny** very small – 10 **shock** *here:* horrible surprise – 10 **to take away one's breath** to stop one from breathing – 12 **to beg** *here:* to ask desperately for sth – 12 **to be in charge of** to be the person who gives the orders – 13 **to struggle** *here:* to fight for one's life – 15 **upset** [ʌpˈset] pulled on to its side (throwing out passengers) – 23 **murmur** [ˈmɜːmə] soft, low sound – 28 **duty** [ˈdjuːti] sth one must do – 30 **to swamp** [swɒmp] to half fill with water

burst, when a rush of hot air pushed him up again. He could see the upturned Collapsible B, and started swimming towards it. At that moment one of the huge funnels crashed into the sea, just missing him and crushing a number of swimmers close by. The wave from
5 the falling funnel carried Lightoller right up to Collapsible B. There were already thirty men lying on it when Lightoller pulled himself on board. The men were pleased to have an officer with them. The boat was getting lower in the water, and the desperate men were no longer able to help each other or anyone else. The icy water was
10 washing over them.

In the meantime, Bride had struggled to the surface and had joined the others. Lightoller now ordered the men to stand up and to balance themselves as best they could. The men obeyed, but one after another the weaker ones dropped off and floated away out of
15 sight …

Most of the women in the boats were soon too cold and miserable to think. Some of them wore nothing but a nightdress and a light coat. They sat very close to one another, trying to keep what little warmth they had. A seaman took off his woollen stockings and gave
20 them to a barefooted woman, adding when she hesitated, "Oh, don't be afraid, Ma'am. They're quite clean."

In some boats women rowed throughout the night, while in boat No. 8, the Countess of Rothes was put in charge of the tiller. The older children were quiet and pressed against their mothers. The
25 babies never stopped crying. Lawrence Beesley covered a crying baby's toes with his blanket and found that he and the child's mother shared a friend in Ireland. Edith Russell kept another baby amused with her musical pig. A twenty-two-year old girl who was half dead with sea-sickness recovered wonderfully when offered her first ever
30 taste of brandy.

The twenty small boats were now scattered over the ice-filled sea. It was still dark, and as cold as ever. In the half-swamped Collapsible

---

11 **to struggle to the surface** ['sɜːfɪs] *here:* to get one's head above water – 12 **to join** *here:* to climb on the boat to be with the others – 13 **to balance** ['bæləns] to try not to fall – 13 **to obey** [ə'beɪ] to do what one is told – 14 **to drop off** to fall off – 20 **barefooted** not wearing shoes or socks – 23 **tiller** ['tɪlə] *Ruderpinne* – 29 **to recover** to get better – 30 **brandy** cognac – 31 **scattered** far away from one another

A a man was dying. The rest, twelve men and one woman, were standing in the boat with water up to their knees. About thirty men had climbed on board, but most of them had fallen back into the sea. If Fifth Officer Lowe had not seen them and come to their rescue, they would all have died …

The remarkable Chief Baker Joughin stepped into the water at 2.20, the last man to leave the *Titanic*. He did not reach upturned Collapsible B until 4.00 a.m. But thanks to the whisky and his determination to live, he was not worried by the cold. There was no place for him on the boat, so he swam alongside until he saw one of his bakers, who let him hold on to him. By the time Joughin was rescued, he had been in the water for over three hours.

The people in the boats began to wonder if they would ever be found. Some of the women began to quarrel with the seamen, calling them 'cowards' and accusing them of taking up places in the boats which their husbands should have had. The seamen, quite rightly, said they had only obeyed orders. In boat No. 8, a Spanish girl, Senora Penasco, who was on her honeymoon, began screaming for her husband. The Countess of Rothes gave the tiller to her cousin, and tried to comfort the hysterical girl. Many of the women knew in their hearts they would never see their men again, but they hid their grief and kept alive a small hope that their husbands and sons had found a place in some other boat. One young man was picked up by his mother's boat, but in the darkness they did not recognise one another. Quartermaster Hitchens was trying to steer his boat to the *Californian*. When he found he could never get there, he gave up hope and said they would all die. Mrs J. J. Brown, a tough, determined millionairess from Denver cried, "Nonsense!" and gradually took charge of the boat herself.

It was a beautiful night. A million stars blazed in the sky. Lawrence Beesley, the schoolmaster, who never lost his powers of observation throughout the long, painful hours, particularly remembered the beauty of the night, and described it romantically in his book.

---

4 **to come to sb's rescue** ['reskjuː] to save sb's life – 6 **remarkable** extraordinary – 14 **to quarrel** ['kwɒrəl] to argue angrily with sb – 20 **to comfort** ['kʌmfət] to calm sb, make sb feel better – 22 **grief** great sadness – 25 **quartermaster** ['kwɔːtəmɑːstə] seaman who steers a ship – 28 **tough** [tʌf] strong, able to fight without fear against great difficulties or dangers

About 3.30, rockets were seen low down in the sky, and not long afterwards a ship's lights appeared over the horizon. The *Carpathia* had arrived. At 4.10 the first of the *Titanic's* lifeboats arrived safely alongside. It was boat No. 2, in the charge of Fourth Officer Boxhall.

As the survivors were lifted on board, the *Carpathia's* passengers noticed there was no joy or excitement on their faces. They were not even talking. The only sound was the crying of a baby. They were quickly taken below, given warm clothes and hot soup and the doctor attended to those who were ill. But the last of the *Titanic's* lifeboats did not reach the *Carpathia* until over four hours later …

One of the Titanic's lifeboats, seen from the Carpathia

When Lightoller and the men still alive on Collapsible B saw the *Carpathia*, they shouted 'Ship ahoy!', but nobody heard them. It was a desperate moment, for they knew they might never be seen. In the growing light they could see icebergs all around them. Fortunately Lightoller had a whistle in his pocket. He blew it, and it was heard at once by seaman Frederick Clinch, in lifeboat No. 12. Clinch could

---

2 **horizon** [həˈraɪzən] line separating sea (or land) from sky – 6 **joy** happiness – 9 **to attend to** to look after – 15 **whistle** [wɪsl] one blows into it. It makes a loud, high sound. Policemen have whistles.

only just see the upturned collapsible in the far distance, but slowly his men rowed towards it, and with great skill took on board the half-dead survivors. Lightoller at once took charge of the boat. It was already 6.30 a.m. when No. 12 began to row towards the *Carpathia*.

5 The boat was overloaded. It was built for sixty-six passengers, but now held seventy-five. The sea was no longer calm, and waves kept crashing against the boat. For a moment it seemed as if it would sink less than 100 metres from the *Carpathia*. Water was pouring in, But Captain Rostron moved the *Carpathia's* bows round to give

10 Lightoller shelter. At 8.30 No. 12, the last boat load, was taken on board the *Carpathia*.

Some of the survivors took a long time to recover. Hundreds of women learned at last that they had lost their husbands. Stewardess Violet Jessop found the mother of the baby she had taken with her

15 in the lifeboat. The mother received it without a smile or a word of thanks. As for Bruce Ismay, as soon as he came on board the *Carpathia* he begged to have a cabin to himself. He refused all food and drink. He wanted to hide his face from everyone.

Captain Rostron decided to take the *Titanic's* survivors to New

20 York. But first he sailed once across the exact spot where the *Titanic* went down. There were bits of wreckage floating amongst the ice, and one dead body, head above water, supported by a white life belt. The Captain was sure that there could be no one left alive.

---

5 **overloaded** too many people on board – 10 **shelter** protection against the wind and the waves – 21 **wreckage** ['rekɪdʒ] bits and pieces left on the surface after a ship has sunk – 22 **supported** *here:* held up with head above the water

9 Judgment

The sinking of the *Titanic* was the sensation of the century. It shook the confidence of the big industrialists. They believed that their skill and their money had at last made the world safe and pleasant to live in – for the wealthy, that is. They did not have much thought for the poor.

It was the poor emigrants from Britain, Ireland and the Continent who suffered most in the *Titanic* disaster. This made many people think for the first time about wealth and poverty and the class system. Third-class passengers watching first-class passengers being lowered in the boats had shouted angrily, 'Millionaires' specials!'. Yet, to be fair to the millionaires, many third-class women were saved because first-class men obeyed the Captain's orders, 'Women and children first!'.

2 **sensation** [sen'seɪʃən] an exciting event – 9 **poverty** being very poor – 9 **class system** a society divided into working, middle, and upper classes, with little mixing between the classes

Left-wing newspapers, churchmen, socialists declared that the disaster was a judgment of God. Among many ordinary people, there was delight that so many wealthy people had died.

"God is not responsible," said a New York priest. "He made man
5 so that he could go out and study His laws. This disaster is the punishment for disobedience of these laws. That iceberg had a right to be where it was, but the ship had no right to be where it was."

Luxury was the goddess of the rich and speed was the Devil. Bruce Ismay was attacked in newspaper articles. He was called a
10 coward and should have gone down with the ship, like Captain Smith. Ismay resigned from his post as managing director of the White Star and retired from public life completely, hiding himself away in a house he bought in Ireland.

There were, of course, Courts of Inquiry on both sides of the
15 Atlantic. Captain Smith was not blamed for the disaster. But the Court added that in future captains guilty of paying no attention to ice warnings would be charged with criminal negligence. The White Star was excused all blame for the terrible losses among third-class passengers, even though it was admitted that stewards had kept
20 third-class passengers below deck until it was too late. But never again in times of emergency would first-class passengers be given preference over third-class passengers.

The part played by the *Californian* was criticised strongly. Officers on the bridge at the time admitted they had seen the *Titanic's* rockets
25 and had informed the Captain. The Captain did not believe they were distress signals. He did not even wake his wireless operator. He turned over and went back to sleep again. One thing appeared certain: if the *Californian* had gone at once to the *Titanic's* help, most of the passengers and crew would have been saved, for she
30 would have arrived long before the *Carpathia*.

Nobody has ever questioned the heroism of the *Titanic's* crew.

1 **left-wing** politically everything to the left of centre – liberal, socialist, communist, marxist – 1 **to declare** to say strongly – 3 **delight** great pleasure – 6 **disobedience** [ˌdɪsəˈbiːdiəns] refusing to obey – 9 **to attack** to criticise strongly – 11 **to resign from one's post** [rɪˈzaɪn] to give up one's job – 14 **Court of Inquiry** a law court which tries to find out why sth happened – 16 **a guilty person** [ˈgɪlti] person who is to blame for a crime – 17 **to charge sb** to say that sb is guilty – 17 **criminal negligence** [ˈneglɪdʒəns] not taking enough care to avoid a disaster – 21 **emergency** a time of danger – 21 **to give sb preference** [ˈprefərəns] to give sb a better chance – 31 **heroism** [ˈherəʊɪzm] behaving like a hero, i.e. with great courage

Only 210 of the 898 members of the crew were saved, and only four of these were officers. All the thirty-six engineers were lost. They worked down in the stokeholds and kept the electric lights going until three minutes before the ship went down. And of the eightyfour stokers on watch, only eight were saved. All the ship's boys were lost. Many of them helped provide the lifeboats with tins of biscuits. The five postal clerks were lost, working until the last minute to bring the mail bags on deck. And of course there was the band – all eight players were lost.

1,502 people died. There had never been such a terrible disaster at sea in peacetime. But the First World War was only two years away, and in this violent and bloody struggle tens of thousands of seamen, of many different nations, were to lose their lives.

The Lessons Learned

- *Wireless:*

  Without Marconi's wonderful invention, wireless, everybody would have been lost on the *Titanic*. If the *Californian's* operator had been on watch, he would have known for certain that the *Titanic* needed help desperately. In future all passenger ships were to have two wireless operators.

- *Lifeboats:*

  Over 1,500 people were left on board, and as the ship went down they had to jump or were thrown into the ice-cold sea. Only about 50 of the toughest (including one woman) survived until they were picked up by one of the *Titanic's* lifeboats. Lifebelts were of no use to the great majority because of the freezing temperature. One of the great tragedies of the *Titanic* was that at least another 500 people could have been saved if full use had been made of the lifeboats. But the most important lesson learned, which in future saved many lives at sea, was that every ship must have enough lifeboat space for every single person on board. It became an international law.

- *Lifeboat drill:*

  It was made compulsory for all ships to have a lifeboat drill.

- *Shipping lanes:*

  Ships were no longer allowed to take the northern route from Europe to New York. The trans-Atlantic shipping route from that day onward was sixty miles further south.

---

13 **lifebelt** *Rettungsring* – 13 **the great majority** [mə'dʒɒrəti] *here:* most of the people – 14 **tragedy** ['trædʒədi] a very sad event – 22 **compulsory** [kəm'pʌlsəri] every ship had to have lifeboat drill

10 Can the *Titanic* be Raised?

For more than 70 years people have believed that the *Titanic* sank as a result of a huge tear in her side caused by an iceberg. It is now known that the collision with the iceberg pushed the steel plates of the liner's hull inwards, forcing out the rivets which held the steel plates together. The plates gave way and the water rushed in. The hull of the *Titanic* broke into two huge chunks.

The man who made this discovery was an American deep sea explorer. In 1986 Dr Robert Ballard and his team found the wreck lying on the seabed more than two miles down. They sailed round it several times in a special deep sea submarine. They saw 'rivers of rust' and millions of skeletons of a certain wood-feeding shellfish that had destroyed the deck and everything else made of wood. But the brass portholes still shone as if they had just been polished.

1 **to raise** to lift – 5 **rivet** ['rɪvɪt] pin holding metal plates together – 7 **chunk** big piece of sth – 10 **the seabed** bottom of the sea

Dr Ballard hoped that the *Titanic* would be left in peace, and he warned treasure hunters that all jewels and other valuables are buried deep under the seabed. He did not believe that the wreck could ever be raised, and he did not bring a single object to the surface.

5 A plaque in memory of those who died was fixed on the stern. It was there that most of the victims stood and waited during the last few minutes of their lives. The plaque reads:

> *"In memory of those souls who perished with the "Titanic" April 14/15, 1912. Dedicated to William H. Tantum, IV whose*
> 10 *dream to find "Titanic" has been realized by Dr. Robert D. Ballard. The officers and members of the Titanic Historical Society inc. 1986"*

Films on the Titanic

There are many films about the Titanic, the first two were made in
15 1912. They were both thought to be lost, but a copy of the German production *"In Nacht und Eis"* was found in 1998. *"Saved from the Titanic"* was made in the USA starring Titanic survivor Dorothy Gibson.

In 1929 the first sound film was made about the disaster; it was
20 called "Atlantic".

"A Night to Remember" is a very accurate film – almost a documentary – made in 1958.

In 1997 the most popular film on the Titanic was made. "Titanic" received 11 Academy Awards (Oscars) and was seen by more than
25 355 million people in cinemas worldwide.

The wreck of the Titanic was the star in "Ghosts of the Abyss" from 2003. It is a 3D documentary investigating the inside of the wreck using special underwater equipment.

9 **William H. Tantum** worked with Dr. Ballard in the 1970s to find the ship.

More maritime disasters

What happened to the other ships mentioned in the book? Most of them travelled the seas for many more years until they were scrapped, but this was not true for two of them.

The *Californian* continued normal service until World War I when the British government took control of the ship. The *Californian* was torpedoed and sunk by a German submarine southwest of Cape Matapan, Greece in November 1915 with the loss of one life.

The *Carpathia* was used to transfer American troops to Europe during World War I and also torpedoed by a German submarine off the east coast of Ireland on 17 July 1918. Five crewmen were lost, while 57 passengers and the surviving crew were rescued by another ship on the following day.

The greatest maritime disaster, with respect to the number of persons lost, was the sinking of the German ship *Wilhelm Gustloff* on 30 January 1945. The *Gustloff* was carrying civilian refugees, German soldiers, and U-boat personnel, when it was sunk by a Russian submarine in the Baltic Sea. 5,348 people are known to have died but it has been estimated that as many as 9,400 may have died as a result of this disaster.

The greatest maritime disaster during peace-time took place in 1987 when the passenger ferry *"Doña Paz"* on her way to Manila (capital of the Philippines) collided with a tanker causing an explosion and fire which spread to the *"Doña Paz"*. Between 4,300 and 4,400 people were killed.

One of history's most famous maritime disaster was the loss of the Italian liner *Andrea Doria*. On her way to New York, *Andrea Doria* collided with an eastward-bound *ship* on 25 July 1956. 1,660 passengers and crew were rescued and survived, while 46 people died as a consequence of the collision.

Looking back further in history, the loss of the *Spanish Armada* stands out. On 8 August 1588, Philip II of Spain sent a large fleet of ships to invade England. Spain lost 15,000-20,000 soldiers and sailors in battles and storms.

11 Persons mentioned in the story. Who died? Who survived?

First-class Passengers

Andrews, Thomas	(Managing Director of Harland and Wolff)	died
Astor, John Jacob	(American millionaire)	died
Astor, Mrs J.		survived
Their French maid		survived
Brown, Mrs J. J.	(American millionairess)	survived
Dodge, Dr Washington	(Tax Officer for San Francisco)	survived
Dodge, Mrs W.		survived
Their son (aged 5)		survived
Sir Cosmo Duff Gordon	(British aristocrat)	survived
Lady Duff Gordon		survived
French maid		survived
Guggenheim, Ben ['gʌgənhaɪm]	(American millionaire – copper mines)	died
Harder, George	(honeymoon couple)	survived
Harder, Mrs G.		survived
Harper, Henry Sleeper	(Harper family owned famous American magazine, Harper's Weekly)	survived
Harper, Mrs H.		survived
Their dog, Sun-Yat-Sen	(Pekingese)	survived
Ismay, Bruce ['ɪzmeɪ]	(Managing Director of White Star Line)	survived
Millet, Frank	(American painter)	died
Penasco, Victor de Satode	(high born Spaniard.	died
Penasco, Senora Victor	honeymoon couple)	survived
Peuchen, Major ['pjuːtʃən 'meidʒə]	(wealthy Canadian)	survived

Rothes, Countess of ['rɔθis]	(British aristocrat)	survived
Rothschild, Martin ['rɒθtʃaɪld]		died
Rothschild, Mrs M.		survived
Russell, Edith	(wealthy American)	survived
Ryerson, Arthur ['raɪəsən]	(American steel magnate)	died
Ryerson, Mrs A.		survived
Ryerson, Jack	(son, 13 years old)	survived
Stead, William	(well-known British writer and journalist)	died
Steffanson, Bjornstrom	(Norwegian)	survived
Widener, George	(American Streetcar magnate)	died
Widener, Mrs C.		survived
Widener, Harry	(son, grown-up)	survived
Mrs Widener's maid		survived
Mr Widener's manservant		died
Woolner, Hugh	(son of an English sculptor)	survived

Second-class Passengers

Beesley, Lawrence	(English schoolmaster)	survived
Caldwell, Albert	(American Missionary teachers)	survived
Caldwell, Mrs		survived
Caldwell, Alden (baby)		survived
Collett, Stuart	(Identity unknown)	survived
Collyer, Harvey	(British	died
Collyer, Mrs Charlotte	emigrants)	survived
Collyer, Marjorie	(daughter, 8 years old)	survived

Third-class Passengers

Buckley, Daniel	(Irish emigrant)	survived
Dyker, Adolf	(Continental	died
Dyker, Mrs A.	emigrants)	survived
Johnsson, Carl		died
Yasbeck, Antoni	(Continental	died
Yasbeck, Mrs Celiney	emigrants)	survived
Woman to whom seaman gave his woollen stockings in lifeboat		died

The Crew

Officers

Captain Smith	died
First Officer Murdoch [ˈmɜːdɒk]	died
Second Officer Lightoller	survived
Fourth Officer Boxhall	survived
Fifth Officer Lowe	survived
Wireless Operator Phillips	died
Second Wireless Operator Bride	survived
Purser McElroy [ˈmækəlrɔɪ]	died
Phillips reached a raft, but [1]died of exposure	

Seamen

Clinch, Frederick	survived
Fleet, Frederick (lookout)	survived
Hitchins, Robert (Quartermaster)	survived
Symons, George (lookout)	survived

1 **to die of exposure** to die from the effects of being outside in very cold weather

Stewards and stewardesses etc.

Hart, John	survived
Jessop, Violet	survived
Martin, Annie	survived
Joughin, Charles ['dʒʌfɪn] (Chief Baker)	survived

There are only few second and third-class passengers mentioned in the book, because the newspapers were only interested in the stories of the distinguished first-class passengers.

Several couples preferred to go down with the ship together. These include three of the first-class women passengers who died.

True or false

Are the following statements true or false?
If they are false, correct the statement. 👍 👎

1 The Titanic was more than 280 metres long. ☐ ☐

2 The Titanic picked up emigrants in France. ☐ ☐

3 There were always many icebergs along the route of the
Titanic at this time of the year. ☐ ☐

4 The Titanic hit the iceberg in the early morning. ☐ ☐

5 There was a great panic after the Titanic had hit the iceberg. ☐ ☐

6 The wireless operators of the Titanic had gone to bed early. ☐ ☐

7 The Californian could have rescued most people on the Titanic. ☐ ☐

8 Some passengers had dogs with them. ☐ ☐

9 Men were not allowed to enter the lifeboats together
with their wives. ☐ ☐

10 There were no seats left free on the lifeboats. ☐ ☐

11 The band played music for the passengers until the
Titanic sank. ☐ ☐

12 The captain was the last person to enter a lifeboat. ☐ ☐

13 At about 4 a.m. the first survivors were picked up by
the Caronia. ☐ ☐

14 More than 2500 persons from the crew and the passengers
died. ☐ ☐

15 The Titanic was found southeast of Newfoundland on the
ground of the Pacific Ocean in 1986. ☐ ☐

Letter grid

Find the ships mentioned in the story

W	M	A	L	M	E	T	C	R	F	P	Y	S	E	W
G	N	H	A	T	K	A	I	N	Q	J	I	P	L	G
C	J	M	X	I	R	J	V	T	E	M	J	X	G	U
A	A	X	E	O	H	H	E	R	A	E	I	N	O	I
G	A	L	N	S	Z	T	O	I	Z	N	N	R	B	S
N	W	I	I	M	A	L	A	L	W	H	I	Y	B	F
I	A	X	K	F	Y	B	D	P	U	J	L	C	R	R
A	O	X	I	M	O	P	A	H	R	C	Z	A	M	D
G	K	E	P	U	Z	R	M	K	Y	A	N	E	G	O
A	S	I	P	Q	M	S	N	D	N	K	C	K	P	O
R	C	F	K	N	O	B	F	I	F	W	R	K	Z	I
A	H	E	R	N	J	C	X	O	A	O	S	C	K	H
Q	D	D	R	M	C	J	R	J	O	N	U	T	Q	V
E	D	W	K	C	D	T	P	O	I	P	O	P	T	K
Q	P	T	G	V	X	R	U	U	I	A	K	P	P	X

1 _____   5 _____

2 _____   6 _____

3 _____   7 _____

4 _____   8 _____

Crossword Puzzle

Complete the crossword

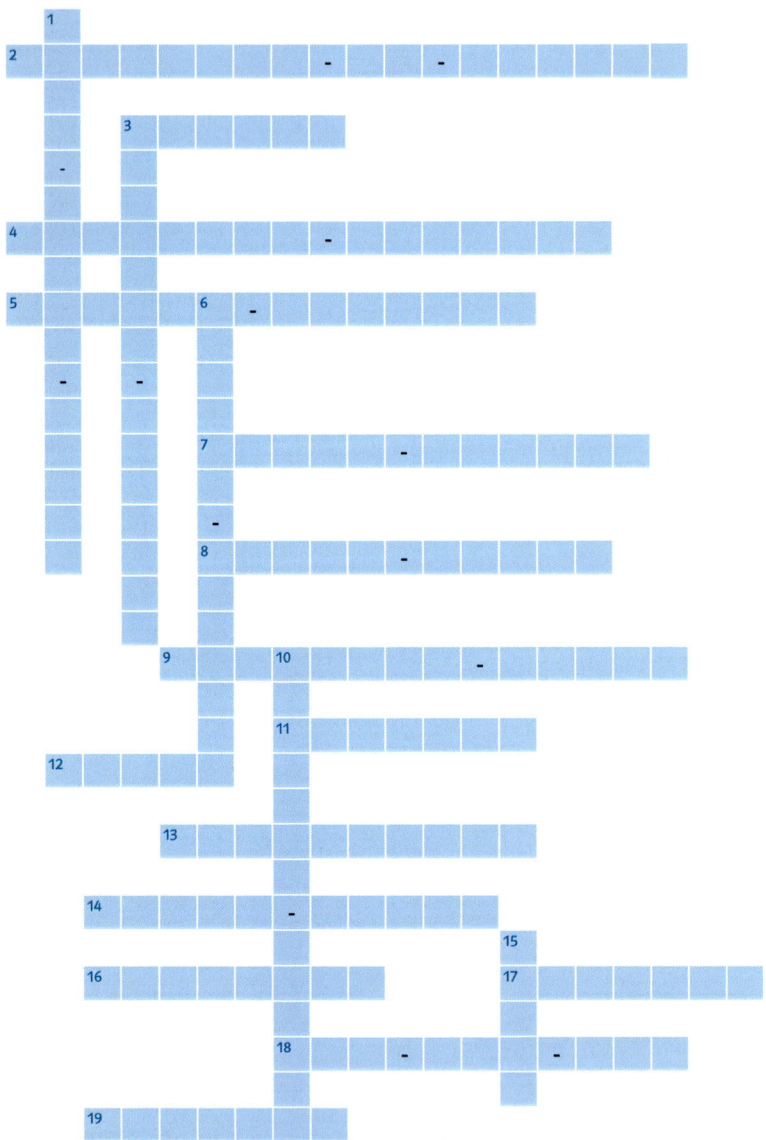

Across:
2 Lady, in charge of the tiller of lifeboat No. 8
3 wireless operator of the Carpathia
4 author of the book called 'The Loss of S.S. Titanic'
5 deep sea explorer
7 stewardess from Portsmouth
8 third-class passenger
9 lookout that first saw the iceberg
11 Captain of the Carpathia
12 the Californian's wireless operator
13 Second Officer
14 managing director of the White Star Line
16 senior wireless operator of the Titanic
17 First Officer
18 peke of Henry Sleeper Harper
19 inventor of the wireless

Down:
1 American multi-millionaire
3 Chief Baker, was rescued after he had been in the water for over three hours
6 Harland and Wolff of Belfast's managing director
10 Titanic survivor starring in the film 'Saved from the Titanic'
15 the Titanic's commander

Photo Credits: